JUN 0 6 2005

WITHDRAWN

Plants That Bite Back

Katy Pike and Paul McEvoy

This hard cover edition first published in 2005
by Chelsea House Publishers

CHELSEA HOUSE
P U B L I S H E R S
A Haights Cross Communications Company ®

Copyright © 2003 Sundance Publishing

This edition of The Real Deal is published
by arrangement with Blake Education.
All rights reserved. No part of this publication
may be reproduced, stored in a retrieval
system or transmitted in any form or by
any other means, electronic, mechanical,
photocopying, recording or otherwise,
without the prior written permission
of the publisher.

Published by
Sundance Publishing
P.O. Box 740
One Beeman Road
Northborough, MA 01532–0740
800-343-8204
www.sundancepub.com

Copyright © text Katy Pike
Copyright © illustrations Paul McEvoy

First published 2002 by
Blake Education, Locked Bag 2022, Glebe 2037, Australia
Exclusive United States Distribution: Sundance Publishing

Design by Cliff Watt in association with
Sundance Publishing

Plants That Bite Back
ISBN 0-7910-8429-9

Photo Credit
p. 20 Geoff Spanner/Auscape

Table of Contents

Trapped! 4
There's no escaping these plants.

A Killer Plant 12
This tree poisons animals.

Call for Backup! 22
Tomato plant gets revenge.

Fact File 30
Glossary 31
Index 32

Trapped!

Plants can't walk, but they can set traps.

Imagine being invited to dinner and ending up as the food. This is what happens to insects that try to feed on plants that eat meat!

Insect Take-Out

An insect looking for food lands on a Venus flytrap. As the insect moves, it brushes against small **trigger hairs**. When it touches these hairs, it's trapped! The trap closes tighter and tighter on the insect. Then the plant digests it.

Venus flytraps live in swamps and **bogs** where the soil is poor. To get enough

Ouch!

Venus flytrap

food, they must feed on the meat of insects. Plants like the Venus flytrap that feed on meat are called **carnivorous plants.**

Hello, breakfast!

Q: What do you call nervous insects?
A: *Jitterbugs!*

A Sticky Death

The sundew is a beautiful plant. Its leaves shine in the sun. Each leaf has hundreds of hairs. Each hair has a drop of sticky liquid on the end. What looks like sweet nectar is really very sticky glue that won't let go!

Insects are attracted to drink the nectar. When they land on the plant, they stick to it. As an insect struggles to get free, the sticky hairs wrap around its body. Now the plant begins to digest the insect's juicy flesh.

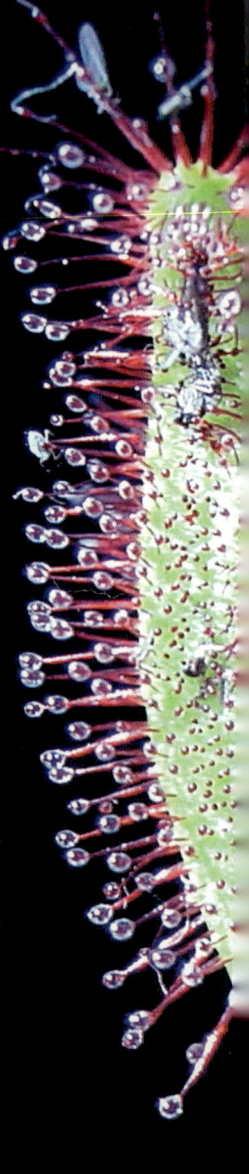

Sundew

Drop In for a Meal

Many plants and insects help each other. When an insect takes a drop of **nectar** from a plant, the insect gets **pollen** on its body. Some of this pollen brushes off onto the next plant the insect visits. This helps the plant to grow new seeds.

Insects that explore the pitcher plant are not so lucky. An insect comes over to taste the nectar. It lands, then it falls down the pitcher plant's slippery slope and is trapped. The insect drowns in a pool of juices. It is now a meal for the plant.

Three types of pitcher plants

A Killer Plant

Plants can't talk, but they can send messages.

Everyone has pulled a leaf from a tree. We think that the tree doesn't notice. But what if the next time you pull a leaf from a tree, it sends the message "Eat my leaves and you'll die!"

That's just what happens to giraffes in Africa.

Here's the Story

Giraffes love to eat the leaves of the acacia (a-kay-sha) tree. First, the acacia tree protects itself with long, sharp thorns. If you were to push one of those branches out of the way, you would get badly scratched!

But the thorns don't stop the giraffes. Their long, tough tongues reach out and eat the leaves anyway. In this hot, grassy land there isn't much else to munch on. That's bad luck for the acacia trees.

Giraffe tongue

Acacia tree

The Plot Thickens

The giraffes don't eat from one tree for very long. They munch away at a tree for a short time, and then they move on.

People watching may think that the giraffe is being nice to the tree. Or they might think that the giraffe is leaving some food for later. The real reason turns out to be very different.

The acacia tree has another way to defend itself—**poison!**

Time to move on for dessert!

Q: What animal makes the most of its food?
A: *A giraffe, because it makes a little go a long way!*

What Really Happens?

1 The giraffe starts to munch on the spiky acacia tree.

2 The tree takes quick action, pushing poison into its leaves.

3. Within 30 minutes, the leaves are too poisonous to eat.

4. This tree sends a message to other acacia trees. They become poisonous as well. The giraffe moves on.

How Do We Know?

A herd of kudu was fenced inside a small area. After eating all of the grass, their only food was some acacia trees. The whole herd of kudu died.

Kudu

So the trees were tested. The results explained why all the kudu died. All of the trees had three times the normal amount of poison in their leaves!

It turns out that at the same time the acacia leaves fill with poison, they release a gas as a signal. Other acacias within 50 yards pick up the signal, and they begin to send poison to their own leaves.

LATER

Call for Backup!

Plants can't run away, but they can send for backup.

A field of plants seems like an easy target if you're a hungry caterpillar. There is so much food in one place. What can a plant do? It can call for help!

The call is answered. Soon the caterpillar is under attack.

Tomato Alert!

The hornworm caterpillar grows big and fat eating the leaves of plants like the tomato plant. Soon it is a juicy, green caterpillar as large as your finger.

It's normal for a caterpillar to grow and change into a moth or a butterfly. The hornworm caterpillar changes into a sphinx moth.

The moth will lay more eggs on the plant. These eggs will hatch into many more hungry caterpillars. But nature has given the tomato plant a way to protect itself. It sends for wasps!

I haven't eaten for five minutes!

Send In the Wasps

Some plants can pump their leaves full of poison, but sometimes this isn't enough. The caterpillars get used to the poison and keep eating.

The plant will be eaten alive. Time to call for backup!

As the caterpillar eats the tomato plant, the plant sends out an odor that acts like a message. When a wasp smells this, it comes flying. The wasp zeroes in and lands on the hornworm caterpillar.

Red alert in tomato sector!

What Happens Next?

1 The wasp lays its eggs on the inside of the caterpillar.

Hey, it's dark in here!

2 When the eggs hatch, the baby wasps (called larvae) feed on the living caterpillar.

We're smarter than we look!

3 When the larvae are ready to change into wasps, they break out of the caterpillar. They spin cocoons and attach them to the outside of the caterpillar.

This stops the caterpillar from changing into a moth. Then it can't produce more hungry caterpillars to eat the tomato plant.

Plants win again!

Fact File

The largest pitcher plant, the rajah pitcher, can hold more than 4 liters (4 quarts) of juice. It can trap frogs and other small animals.

If a caterpillar ate the African bugleweed, it would grow two heads when it became a butterfly! Then it would die.

This way!

There are thousands of poisonous plants. Some have strange names like bloodroot, hemlock, poison ivy, and deadly nightshade.

The sap of milkweed is so poisonous that it can give small animals a heart attack.

Glossary

bog an area of land that is always wet and spongy, made up of decaying plants

carnivorous plant a meat-eating plant

larvae the young of an insect

nectar a sweet liquid produced by flowering plants

poison something that can kill people or animals if it is swallowed or absorbed

pollen a fine, yellow powder made by flowers

trigger hairs hairs that when touched cause a plant's leaves to close

Index

acacia tree 14–21

African bugleweed 30

carnivorous plants 4–11

giraffe 12–19

hornworm caterpillar 24–29

kudu 20–21

milkweed 30

pitcher plant 10–11, 30

poison 17–21, 30

sundew 8–9

tomato plant 24–29

Venus flytrap 6–7

wasp 26–29